The 13th Secret Code

Sosé Gjelaj

TABLE OF CONTENTS

Time

Once again, no time.
No time to get anywhere.

Do we play like fools?
And often we talk to ourselves?
What if time was a witness?

Or do we always feel like
we are falling Angels?
Can we find out
where we are going?

Suppose we should ask
Who are we?

A small rock.
A desert.
Emptiness,
emptiness.

2004

Voices

Sometimes,
when I close my eyes,
I hear a voice.
But I do not understand it,
I do not understand the language.

And this red mirror
stands in front of me.
I look closely into it
and I see the absence of pleasure,
the absence of time.

I forgot to breathe.
I juggle between sadness and the sun.
The fire is floating somewhere inside.
And I hear a child's cry.
I hear I sleep in deep meadows

But it doesn't really matter.
These are just stories,
only stories that
my mind creates.

2004

The Streets of New York

Once I passed by a church...
I saw an Angel.
This Angel was in a long limousine,
on the streets.
He was wearing a mask,
looking at the fools in the crowds.

Where are these heroes?
What would become of them?
Have they lost their voices?

Perhaps we all drink
too much Champaign.
To mask our illusions,
we enter with a password.

Everyone migrates,
including the birds in high roofs.
What have we forgotten?
Call me.
And the noise dangles to the veins.

Improvise, pull the curtain,
play, play, Universe.

The world of entering.
Oh well...

Children play with illusions.

2004

Not Being

We can't be afraid to write.
Words are words.
Grammar is for fools.

I understand -
the hat,
the cet,
the balluun,
the dans,
the airr,
the suun,
the muhn,
the mornink.

2004

Earth's Thunder

Ah, the fire, the thunder...
Suddenly, we learn to speak
with a sustaining apple
and a cigarette in our mouths.
The dark rings under our eyes.

Hidden passages,
composing the future.
But I really do not care.
In a long distance,
an Angel stares in shadows.
I can see him,
smiling, whispering.
Don't run, stop this illusion,
because the heart is still beating.

It is like swimming in a large ocean.
If not careful, you lose direction.
So drunk with pain...
Should I tell the story?

Silence is the death
that dangles in shadows
like the black widow dancing in a grave.
The silhouette draping the wings of woe.
Maybe the Earth is watching...

The body is filled with hope.
Where does time begin?

And where does it fall after I awake?

1999

Connection

When I am connected,
the world is different from above.
And I truly like it that way.
Everything is possible.
The feeling of happiness,
the feeling of sleeping
on an Angel's wing.

Someone is listening to my thoughts,
smelling the perfume that I am wearing
which still lingers in the air.
Then I run.

I feel a tingling and a ticking.
I feel my heart beating,
but I am so involved in looking,
looking for a name.

"I feel you in here,
please touch my hair.
Are you a falling Angel in my bed,
in the edge of my shallow light?"
He whispers gently...

I can feel, I can feel him.
I can feel the feet on the ground
in a cold, cold winter rain.
And the red color of my dress.

And the drink of my desire
in my hand.

Is it a matter of a chance?
Or is it the opposite of my embrace?

1987

Mystery of Love

Sometimes by chance,
strangers meet in the far distant land.
It is not fitting somehow.

And in that moment,
the face is covered with light.
The dust seems to
have evaporated in the air.
But I don't mind.

I can still see from a long distance
the frame of your desire
penetrate through the misty rains.

No Date

Reflections of the Past

I want to see it move
as graceful as a gentle butterfly,
side by side with clouds of motion
and in the shores of the sea.
I feel the waves,
the little droplets on my face.

Oh Spirit,
I drift marveling in the colors in your hair,
I struggle to remember the great Magician,
dissolving into a rose,
shifting one form into another.
I watch the dark sky become thick with clouds.
And then I look down on Earth
in this light flowery valley,
in this ancient forest.

And in a distance, I see a bridge.
Underneath lay a peaceful lake.
Across this lake, a giant tree
stood tall with its magnificent beauty.
There you sat waiting and as I got closer,
the dim shade in the darkness
penetrated through my soul.

Could I be certain?
Who are you?

Who am I?

No Date

Our Giants

One by one rising to power,
gaining sophistication.
Such possibilities of hope.
Now, can we please sit down
and talk together?

Ask me a question,
ask me about the meaning of life.
What was the hardest?
Ask if I was happy.
Oh, what the heck,
ask me if I am Mona Lisa.
Or ask me if I am a dream.
Or ask me if we are dreaming.

Here, in truth, evolution occurs.
It only seems logical, metaphysical.
It is a very possible,
spontaneous composition,
where the lanterns are lid
to make wave for tomorrow's God.

I am hearing you now,
the sound of the flute.
And at the same time, believe me,
the creator's approach,
with starling eyes.

Can we obtain peace?

Here lay the face of adversity,
here lay the face of hope,
the dizzy spell in perpetual motion.
Beyond any expectation,
pulling it at the chest,
the only thing that keeps us alive.

Let's take it to the ocean
and there we would give away
our despair.

September 24, 2008

Hell Hotel

People's oppressed minds,
cunning, deceiving.
They are ignorant.

This is how the strong
invades the weak.

Incapable rulers,
Nations' lost advantage,
deviating from the momentum
of nature.

2006

Uncertain Beginnings

Only through agitation
peace is attained.
Great form carries us
with great mass.
In repeated prays
there is no praise.

I shall close the door
and shut my eyes
to this cursive mind.
I will return to eternal essence,
to eternal Love.

A small fry does not stir much.
It is a paradoxical saying.
The director is present,
the strings of marionettes lie
in the hands of Gods and Goddesses.

Truly logic suppresses
the artistic mind.
To truly restore order from chaos,
we need wisdom.

Confusion arises from war.
It is pulling the roots,
leaving the branches to rot

for accessible wealth

and easy style.

July 1, 2006

She

She looks in the distance,
but she cannot see
the world of illusions.
To here, everything is real.

What am I?
Who am I?

Am I a creature from the sky?
An Angel sent by heaven?
Ah, accept things as they are.

Fears and illusions
trapped in conclusion.

No Date

Cassandra's Song

Am I my body?
My body is mine.
Is it me?
Is it free?

The sound,
the clown,
the seven steps
to take to be born.

Fire in the belly,
water in the head.
The serpent gently rolled
to smell the rose
in a white cloud
through a golden gate.

I wait by the candle
for the blue bird.
But then,
the orange moon
fades away.

November 3, 2001

Stone

Loosing contact with God
feels like a stone.

In a deep black night,
emerge of solution.

Perhaps in a shorter distance
lies a blink.

November 3, 2001

Momentum

Shallow is a river.
It flows through our feet.
We extend our hands
in a tiger sleeping motion.
Bliss.

November 3, 2001

Message

I have walked behind the shadow.
Everything is here.
I have touched the rainbow,
but everything is here.
I have touched the star,
but everything is here.
I have swum in a deep ocean,
but everything is here.

Here I am, inside of you.
You are inside of me.
That's the way it was
and that's the way
it will forever be.

November 3, 2001

Hearts

Revelations happen.
Stop not there...
there is a golden flower.

Long microphone
awaits in the corner.
The violin plays in the distance.
William Faulkner's mind
will tell you so.

Live by your sense,
live in the present.
Save the planet,
speak with your heart.

No Date

Internal Dialogue

Through conflict,
we learn about ourselves.
Through sorrow,
we learn about life.
From life,
we learn to love.
Through love,
we find God.
Through God,
we learn eternal truths.

No Date

Going Home

The wind of change is coming.
I bowed down
and cried me a river.

I laid down my heart
to the tremble of Earth
where my soul soared
to the beaming of the light.

Night turned into day,
day turned into night.
I watched it go...

I dreamed myself
into the tomorrow.
I let myself breathe
the scent of Earth.

March 6, 2005

Moments

She used to sit on his lap.
His hand will slowly caress
her spine downward.
Sand would drift
between his fingers.

It wasn't the sand
of the sun worshipers
seeking a golden opulence.
But it came in cold, hard clumps
breathing the frigid air.

The solid rock behind them
resembled the unspoken words.

October 29, 2002

John

I dream about
what it would be like
to look into your sad eyes
and see the wide world in them.

I guess it makes me sad to think that
there is never going to be a first time.

And this sudden stillness
in your gaze, the warmth
of your encircling
arms.

It is not me, it is you...
Here I am, caught in the hazy sun.

How do I feel?
After all, I am a Montenegrin
and sometimes I like the thunderstorm.

But this is idealistic world
and matters not much to me.

January 28, 2008

Desire to Rest

When we are exhausted,
we put power into a negative thought.
When we desire to rest.

In achieving something into our lives,
we undertake our means,
we use our strengths,
we expand our thoughts
into different directions...
and bankrupt our power.

The next day we dread
the demands of proportions.
We feel lost in our fatigued bodies,
in the hearts of life difficulties
and life's struggles.

So then when we lay down to rest.
Our bodies and minds wander
in the opposite direction.
The sense of responsibility.
It takes a different shape.

Even as we speak,
our nervous system
and physical conceptions
stand still.

February 22, 2002

Now

And now is the moment
to listen to the silence
while I tear the dream apart,
hugging with the rush of dawn,
the shape of things to come.

No Date

Arabian Moment

Is this a bad dream
that unfolds the summer night?

I embrace the silence
and the shadows
that creep inside my mind.

I asleep beneath the cloud
and over the hills,
covered in the misty rain,
leaving no address to outer space.

The wind has turned its force
against the wall where
the little creatures crawl.

May 11, 1988

Lover

Owl shall fling up into the air,
but shall be overtaken unaware
to grasp the scheme of things entire.

Remolded nearer to the heart's desire,
I awake from mornings in slumber.
Once departed, return no more.

The New Year is awakening
all desires, music of a distant drum.

It's for those who fling
the wings of rain
on the river's lips which we lean
from one's lovely lips unseen.

May 12, 1988

Dedicated to God

Oh my Beloved,
fill the cup
that clears today's regrets
and the fears of the future.

I may be in that tune
of internal being of loveliness
into the ocean of bliss.

Walking on the flower
that blooms forever
and in the magic
of the unseen.

May 12, 1988

Rivalry

How long of infinite pursuits
to dispute the rule?
A line that fades things entire.

We shatter into bits
and then remold ourselves
nearest to the heart's desire
where the soul sleeps
like a teddy bear.

They stabbed our hearts
and it deepened the pain
in the eyes.

Do you remember
of how all of a sudden
you smile to yourself
and you clutch your head
closer to your breast?

I will live,
again and again.

May 12, 1988

Wonderment

A holy tent with a huge glittering
in a night of stars.
Ah, but the brain of hopeless,
all of mine.
Watch my body walk.

Wonderers wonder in my brain.
How can my heart explain?
It misses a beat to a thought
and how sweet it is,
it does not seem to be its part.

I hear it running,
the wonder of the plays.
Live in color and live in me,
print ourselves in glass
in the waves of light.

No Date

Prophets

The wine of life
keeps oozing,
drop by drop.
Lives keep falling,
one by one.

Glorious of this world,
prophets' paradise to come.
Treasure in the garden.

No Date

Rays of Light

The hinges of wheels
are traversing
the golden rays of light.

Different directions.

North, through the narrow winding roads
like the changes of musical notes.
A symbolic presence,
manifesting itself
into the inner eye.

In some faraway place,
a shadowy fairyland.
letting the mind run to the mansions,
marked by time.

Is this a question
or is this a doubt?

The foreign energy slips through
your personal world,
disturbing the silence.

Now that you are awake,
the ghostly presence stands for a moment
in a shadow between a window and a door.

No Date

Autogenesis

Money drain rather money gain.
We are hypnotized by
the patterns of human spheres.

We are born liberated,
but live in metaphors,
reflected in broken mirrors
where our reflections
play tricks with our
beautiful minds.

Peace and war lay in
the center of gravity.

We rise from a deep sleep
into internal delight
in the arms of God
where the Universe
is always beginning now.

February 29, 2002

Stranger

As strangers we meet
and as strangers we leave.
Indeed foreigners.

Children of God,
victims of wrong done,
breaking the sounds of music,
the dialogue labored by time.

A true lover grazing
the glorious hopes
that lay behind.

Are we satisfied?
Generating within a place
which we are reborn,
corresponding to objective thought,
reflecting what we once
knew before.

Did we go so far
by breaking the law
of love's pure heart?
Weren't we once friends?

Perhaps I am dreaming
or perhaps this is just

a place in time.

No Date

Timelessness

Walking between worlds,
it's like walking through a TV screen.
Going from one passage into
the mysterious worlds of our minds.

The web of transformation,
so many and yet one self.
Sharing thought into
some invisible mind,
taking us in circles.
A tranquil force
confronting us in silence.

Perhaps a gentle mist
that sweeps the sweet smoke
by digging from inside of a deep memory
that has been lost and forgotten,
breaking the silence chambered
inside of our flesh.

January 24, 1999

Perceived

Here's the sacrament of forgiveness
and the door of pains.
Open it so I can feel
that we are truly alive.

Like the opposites,
reflecting the human consciousness,
it is the matter of spirit,
a matter of nature
joining in harmony.

The spiritual physical union,
a flower growing every spring
from year to year.

A fulfillment.
An identity.
An affirmation.

January 26, 1999

Followed

I walked and he followed.
The voices behind
were whispering.

He coiled his body around
a mystifying dream.
His eyes were crystallized,
colors of fire,
dragging his slow body
into a shape.

There he was standing still.
And his footsteps echoing
through internal walls
of his flesh.

No Date

Interpretation

South away onto the deep,
it leaves the mind into the steep
where thoughts are passing
a river door.
This is where dragons send forth
breaths of fire,
conversations in sweet desire.

Watching the days of prosperity,
under the shallow stream.
But I don't know this recipe.
The wise would stay aroused.

It's written in the old songs.
But this is not the time
of the yester years.

Here we are -
in divinity.

July 28, 1999

Why?

There's no doubt
that we shall feel love,
overshadowed by doubt,
waiting for the adventure's fire
where the wild is still wild,
waiting to kiss its rose.

Man striving forward.
What voice speaks
in a moon stone
where all smiles
echoes across this valley,
calling the flame of magic rings.

Behind the river's flow,
come to mountain's arms,
further on midnight rose.

Old memories untold
for the moment
of needless fear.
Feathers must fall.

No Date

Manhattan

A traveler traveling from BC,
the seven wonders of twelfth century,
the constellations of towers and spire,
the tower of Manhattan's,
a beatify of chariot's desire.

A giant telescope,
a lunar probe,
gleaming beetles between cars.
Neon signs through a pedaled rose,
windows embraced in emerald and in gold.

The night's spots gather
to begin an evening's play.
A tower of Babel,
a skyscraper,
Brooklyn Bridge intertwined
into a wired rope
and people filled with hope.

Glamour walks on Madison,
Central Park fills the music in the air,
museums are filled with ancient treasure.
It is all for the human pleasure.

July 29, 1999

Between Lines

In this epic poem,
hungered for the tears
and unborn love.
It was a time from a deep ocean
where impulses grow.

This is where the warriors
liberate themselves from terror.
This is the generous passion.

Is this a flame or is it a taboo?

No Date

Diva

As the serpent hissed,
a dark river opened.
Under a huge mirror of the Universe,
caught reflections of the illusions.

She dissolved herself into the water,
becoming the liquid of delight
and then her ribs spread far
into Earth.

No Date

A Prayer

There is a church
in the hills of Moldavia.
Its walls painted
in the sunset violets hues.

In the deep chapel,
they bow in prayer,
endless in procession.

Christ rises
in the triumph of passion
and the eyes return to the viewer.

A glimpse of eternity
into thy flesh.

No Date

Traveler

Close your eyes
to the sounds
of instrumental strings.

Motions echoing,
roaring oceans of distant thunder.
Giant monsters of our mind.

No Date

To Francis Golffing

Far away from the hills
we will watch the sinking sun,
drinking the depths of night.

Should we join the soul
of the Universe?
Will we know strength?
Or will we wait
and watch till dawn?

This foretells in the beauty soft,
gentle of life's fire.
Rise and say:
"Shall we dance?"

No Date

New Age

By the sun,
into these hidden worlds,
we lit the fire
to the bottom of the well.

And in these stolen moments,
empty old books,
imitations,
phone numbers without faces.

This endless waiting
awakens the restless light.
Hope keeps belly full in faith.

Showering the sun
in the eyes of time,
drawing lines in computer times,
we are in this movement
of untruth untold,
in the winds of whisper
to this paradise unfold.

No Date

A Reflecting Moment

The rain outside is dripping
through the veins of my soul.
I am here, sitting by a window
in this cold, cold night,
sipping my tea.

A small mirror on the table.
I reach forward,
but my reflecting tired eyes
and my mind so weary.

And there's a half-eaten
cookie on my plate.
And my dog is curled by my feet.
I wonder what he is dreaming.

A torso of a guitar in the corner
waiting to be played.
My hat is hanging by the fire
and my mind is wondering.

No Date

Michelle

Uncertain stride breaks.
Forever cast into echoes.

Take a moment
to tiny blossom
if we are lucky.

Perhaps a tiny stone
on our path,
we will discover
love again,
thing to obtain.

November 17, 2000

Silent

In silence our mind wonders.
Further out it sweeps the wind
in a style of a hue,
as calm as glass.

In tomorrow's promises
shall rise like the sun,
colored by afternoon's rose.

And then quiet is broken.

November 20, 2000

Warrior

I have been giving
a moment of living,
surrounded by moonlight sky.
The haunting from long ago
was like the feathers and the snow.

You say the moments that we share
will never fade away.
Will night change
and seasons pass by?
Would you be thwarted
by the belly of the beast?

Dear Warrior,
give your sward a rest,
come sleep in my chest.

You say you are guided
by the shadow of the moon,
walking by a shore.
But what are you looking for?

No Date

To Michelle

What must I do to let go of you?
What must I say?
Can we ever let go?
Attachments that are so deep.
Maybe I will.

You will fly high
like a feather in a snow,
a pondering rose
in a tiny island.
Or perhaps a tiny pebble
in a large ocean,
drifting from the waves,
taking you from land to land.

And these winds whisper in my ear.
I hear you calling me:
"Mommy, mommy, I love you!"
I hear your voice
and it sends music to my ears.
The presence of you
dominates the room within a glow.

Your beauty is so deep,
poets cannot describe.
I know I must let go,

because I can smell you in the room

and the presence of perfume.

July 7, 2001

War

The face of war
becomes hideous in the
vast oceans of our minds.

People are caught
in a ring of emotions
that penetrate the hate through
as bulls in an arena.

February 14, 1999

Darling

As I moved through this empty house,
a strong wind swept upon me,
leaving me in this perpetual motion.

Slowly I journeyed towards the sunlight,
next to a fountain, to drink.
The reunion of my spirit left me,
everything became a distant memory,
delighting in the agreeable feeling
that filled me and then left me empty.

The details of inside battle,
running inside my chamber.
It is present like an animal in a cage.
We viewed the world
in its marvelous treasures,
waiting to be discovered.
We dared to dream.

The language of the heart,
intense love,
moments that consume
the one who loves
leaves me in a dizzy spiral.

What is the secret?
Is this the language of the mind?
Logic?
Or was it the soul's secret code?

I know this language too well.
By seldom do I hear it.
And in this amazing moment,
I watched the manifestation
of Eros dance around us,
jumping into others'
transforming heart of emptiness.

The power of love lays
in the work we do.
And that trickery arrows
shows its most beautiful face,
united with arrows and Philos
in this divine spark,
in an impressive river,
in search of a secret love.
In that moment,
love consumes,
it makes everything else
less important.

It turns aggression into dust,
enthusiasm towards goals.
You and I were in that divine flame.
And in that moment,
we wanted to change the world.

2008

To Michelle (The Alian)

I carried three pregnancies –
one in my mind,
one in my heart
and one in my soul.

She is like the sea rich in depth,
like the tide that runs a shore.
Blessed is the mother,
blessed is the father,
blessed are the humans
of her beautiful smile.

Her long legs reach to Zenith,
the face of a Goddess,
a paintbrush cannot paint.
Her beauty is the essence
of her perfume.
She is a woman
of many desires.

She is my mantra,
she is my bliss,
she is the comedian of my heart.
I am so grateful she chose me
to be her mama.

February 2, 2009

My Mother

What is morality?
Is it a voice of conscious
in a smoky passage?

She lays in a splendid grass
where flowers grow.
Oh, dear God,
how I miss her so.
She is a very distant memory
that lays low in my heart.

Her petit body lays in the
mountains of Montenegro,
held by the mother Earth.

She is so far that
no one brings her flowers.
But she is in a peaceful place
where eagles fly high,
birds ricochet,
flowers grow
and rivers run through.

And in my dreams,
I visit her from time to time.
Her favorite flower is a white daisy
so she would wear it in her hair.

Tears run from the memories of you.

The touch of your hand I yearn.
My dear Mother,
sleep in the light that never ends.

February 10, 2009

Oliver (Michelle's dog)

He is the ever-present,
the cosmic river,
omnipresent light.

His eyes are the mirror
which reflects back at me
in all forms and colors
without changing
my own nature.

When I see him,
I melt in him
like the heat melting
different metals,
uniting them in one.
I dissolve into a bliss.

He loves me without judgments.
His love digs into the ground
perhaps to sculpt Eva.
His toys give him pleasure,
but his mother's Love
gives him joy.

No wonder
kings and queens love him.
You are magic...
The vastness of your eyes
carry rhythm.

Where did you come from?

When you visit me,
you sleep with me.
You abandoned your mother
for your grandmother.
Your original nature
opens the luminosity in my soul.

You are the light,
the space within space.
You are just is-ness.
You are Love.
You are my grandson.

February 2009

Ambrosia

When metaphysical visions
vanish into inner space,
the experience of heart's desire.
For without it,
the mysterious has no meaning.

Desire is a pure pleasure.
Is the goal fulfilled?
So fly into the matrix sky
and vanish.

October 2, 2009

Fear

Fear,
perhaps it is an illusion.
It sits in a dark corner
somewhere deep in our minds.
At the same time,
it's reaching to speak
the worlds of the unknown.

Silence is always present
in the moment.
And it's inside somewhere,
looking through a hole
to reach to the top.

And then the unconscious
grabs fear by hand.

February 7, 1992

What is Loneliness?

We all gather in groups
for the same deep desires
to free ourselves
from these deep, deep,
dark corners of our minds.

It's like this dark sister,
attached at the ribs,
crying desperately
for the separation.

February 27, 1997

The Noble Cat (Dedicated to Fehu)

From the pharaohs of Egypt,
to the Sphinx of Gita.
The sun of God Ra
into the celestial lions
of the moisture and the air
that is held by the sun,
that is held by the sky.
To the sons and daughters,
separate not from the Earth.

We are the Gods of the Earth
and the disks of the Sun.
We sometimes disappear
from the mountains of the West
and reappear over
the mountains of the East.

We are the gods and goddesses
of music and magic.
Dancing into the distant rainbow,
the Guardians of sleep
and the bridge of dreams.
And then, this magical time
of unending joy.

We are like the Goddess Basted.
We beat out the rhythm
of joy and pleasure.

We are sacred to Leto
who gave birth to Apollo.
We are that, we are magic.

April 28, 1997

The Gulf of Mexico

Sometimes the unseen world
is the real world.
And it is sitting, waiting
in beneath of a surface
of a life of joy,
of the small things
and large
and of the hard
and of the soft.

Our body is the water of life.
And it's sustaining the changes
of the ocean wave of oneness.
And as I listen to it speak
of its secret knowledge
like a child
listens to its mother.
Or a mother listens to its child.

This womb of the Universe
explodes in waves ageless
as time dancing the dance
beyond the unbroken flow.

July 5, 1997

Interconnectedness

Dante's paradise
in the eyes and in divine,
in heavenly body.

The expanse of space surrounding the Earth,
the stars above the clouds and winds
and the green Earth
and the ocean blue.
The mountains high
and the streams below.
And the animals running free
and children dancing
with flowers in their hair.

They are dancing into the new Golden Age.
They hold hands with the young and old
to bring freedom and love a chance,
to connect all nations to be free
so that we can all live in this unity.

To set all children free,
to dance in harmony.
And this is the way
heaven will be.

No Date

The Dragon Dance

Violin playing in his breath,
His heart beat produced the drum.
Lost in some trance of harmony,
I danced and he danced with me.
My soul lingered in the distant sun,
producing violent rays.

Oh boy,
This put me in the days.
This was unity by some destiny.
Perhaps a law of oneness,
of great mystery,
reaching inside my soul,
discovering the harmony
of all creation.
He gives me advice
on every question.

The monster of magic and mystery.
Let our children be free.
I danced and he danced with me.
My hands were moving in slow motion
like some spirit in passion.

The shadows in the cave were so large,
In truth I had no explanation
Or was this just a reflection?
I danced in the present
I danced the past,

I danced the future.
The present needs changing
or modifying.
The future looks grandifying.
Pursue to create the truth,
passion and desire
or equal in creation.
Let my feet on the ground
so I will not drawn.

He said: "Come back and dance with me,
I promise I will give you a key,
please come back and visit me".
A tear was large in his eye
as he said: "goodbye".
Dragon, my friend,
Dragon, my partner,
I shall find the magic gate again,
I shall dance into your heart, my friend.
Bring the box back, filled with mystery
and for me to see,
I shall set the ocean free,
but please, please, please
come back and dance with me.

May 22, 1997

Narrow Window

The forsaking dreams
of gentle shadows
and the light that lets me free
into the darkness
to hide her feeling of distress.
Lower down to the stairway
that dissented into the narrow window.
the light expanded into
the distant walls behind.

The echo of her mind
became a theatre in a hasty room
where spiders now
make their nest.

And if her heart
became the servant of a stranger
and she walks like a shadow.
This is the mystery of solitude,
the lonely traveler.

No Date

The Passing Hour

I hear the sound of a bell
that strikes as the hour passing
second by second.
Here in the village,
here's the drowsy house
and here I am
listening to the hallow murmur.
Announcing the coming
of traveler moving through time.

I stop for a moment
Or was it an hour
or was it a century?
I could not tell.
It seems as though I heard
the sounds of a sleepless soul,
wondering like myself
for a spell.

Here in deep reverie,
questioning life's desire
on this borrowed time.

No Date

The Forgotten Past

To pears through the mind
and its arrival
at the eternal journeys
where the thought began
into another thought.

Illusions to be discovered
that were hidden
in the pendulum clocks
in its tone awakened strike.

It was hidden
in this magical circle.
It frightened me
to the despair
of my imagination's power.

We are complete,
but forgotten.

No Date

The Dream

The winding roads
of our journeys,
of the paradoxes.

And through the eyes
of the dreaming body,
awakened by the mask of the sun,
we enter here
with the sense of vague
of our own eternal beauty.

And these unforeseen mirrors
hung on walls,
touching the face
that confronts us all.

But these crystalline forms
of China dolls
and the Gods that walk with us
make this dream
a pleasant one to be in.

October 1998

Phantom

My past became like
the painting of Dolly
where past, present, future
became illusions.
But at that moment
I live free of thought.

No Date

Shift of Consciousness

One must reach beyond the illusions,
beyond themselves,
beyond the Universe,
beyond the planets
and beyond time.

No Date

Awareness

To listen,
to truly listen,
one's mind must be quiet
and that's where
true understanding
of truth is observed.

No Date

No Name

Children of light
smile with the face of Buddha
with a large stomach filled with
harmony.

No Date

Jump

The scientists wrote to the rose,
pleading to respond
to the sun's bright color
so he can feed the plant cells.
Instead he fed himself to symbols,
Metaphors and profound theories.

Like poets who invent connections,
like the spirit who connects
with body and soul,
he flew into the dream world
of his own making.
And this is where he invents
amplifications of his desire.

But somehow his yard stick mended
and then nature of reality
took a different shape.
His mirror of his observation
reflected back to his assumptions.

So he shines light to it,
the light dances swiftly
and then strikes the eyes
with energy's reaction
in a form of an ocean wave,
creating his own reality.

No Date

Hangover

Once in this luminescent dream
comes forward
like smoke from a burning of a cigarette.

And when you are on the street,
you watch how they walk in a trance.
Some walk in these deep illusions,
some just ignore it all.

They run to the bar -
give me vodka,
give me gin,
give me wine,
give me back my broken soul.

Absolute reality
in an absolute distress.
Here we are,
all drinking the drink of delight
and then the next day
we wake up with a hangover.

August 29, 2002

La Bella Luna

Gazing through night-mist.
The whispers of dusky creatures
which gaze at me
through the frosted light,
bathe in heavenly glint.

Hypnotized by the mirrors of time,
translucent images of my mind.

No Date

The Dining Room
in the Haunted White House of Wilmington

As I walk down the stairs,
there is a window facing
with bright late afternoon glow.

Standing there like a bride
waiting for her groom,
stranger was walking
right behind me.
I can feel his breathing flowing
like silk ribbons flying
across the sky.
And in a momentarily sect,
I was downstairs where the host
was greeting us.

As we step into the dining room,
two tables were occupied
with lovers sharing their secrets.
I can hear a woman laughing
next to the fireplace.
She was so taken by her love,
she herself was lost in
her own dream.

As I looked around the dining area,
I can see the waitress is coming forward,
but she was walking so slow.

It was like a motion movie
that was made in Yester years.

She says: "Good evening,
may I start you off with a drink?"
And for that moment,
I looked passed her across the room.
Through another door I heard jazz music.
It was slowly getting louder
where Stranger and I were sitting.

And with the blink of an eye
I saw shadows of people
men and women
dressed in elegant clothing
From Yester years.
From a dream, sitting in reality,
I stare.
I was lost in some far away time,
but in this time
I can smell the perfumes,
colognes of lovers dancing beside me
and my soul just lingered.

Was I projecting the stage
of ancient theatres?
Containing the actors of time,
translating an image,
a passage
in another language
only to find that I am there.
I feel pain on my toes

87

as if it was coming
from some far away journey.
I am back.

Stranger is staring.
The waitress is staring at me.
And he said: "Please, please, please,
don't go away, come back!"

No Date

Kosovo

In bewildered strings,
lost in a musical note,
a lion stood hollowing
in front of an Angel.

In some corner of the world
lovers were caught
in some mystical illusion.
And perhaps in some train stations,
posters hung beyond the empty walls
and closed windows.

A desk in the corner,
head bow down thinking.
In these subdivided triangles,
a giant step confronting man
in the four corners
leap in different directions.
And in that moment
the night and day stand still.

They all gathered in prayer,
the young, the old
in this perpetual dark mountains
waiting for the red and white blue ribbon.
Or perhaps a child playing with a kite
in all the voices of hunger?

And all the blessed fish

and the promise so that God
can throw down the rain for hope.

No Date

Kundalini

The serpent curled itself
up into the fresh blossoms
of Eva's breast.
Night fell, the moon conceived the
birth of language.

She awoke and the sun blinded her eyes.
She looked down on the serpent's elixir.
She rooted down into the ground for comfort
and there she brought forth
the breath of life.

No Date

To Francis

The summer drifts through a leaf,
carrying oceans of rain.
All of the embraces -
a table, a dish, a dog, a cat, a glass of wine,
smoking a pipe and cigarettes.
The rocking chair squeaks and moans.
We don't care,
we are flicking our ashes into the floor,
waiting to see who is at the door or on the phone.

Did we speak lines of epic poetry,
describing all the colors we could not see
and sometimes wear these words of magic?
Or is it a reflection in the mirror of our desires?
Were we celebrating divinity
or holding on to the fire of memory?

Not a moment of regret,
the devil holds hands.
Now that we are alone,
carrying us into the recollection of drifting,
falling and rolling
and then whispering gently.
Composing mathematically.

1998-1999

Warrior

We thrive to grasp
negative misunderstanding.
Rest upon diversity
between ego and emptiness.

These monuments built by man
are an escape through the walls
of an illusion where logic is enchanted.

And the garden filled with jewels,
hide behind a smoky cloud.
Our passes and parades
are always running through
and sometimes the inner light
is frightened.

No Date

The Cry of the Wild

The symbols of our minds
trapped in memory of our times.
And if we can only see
through the eyes of destiny,
we would no longer cry.

But these egos
that are flying so high.
Why?
Is it in the name of freedom
or in the home of love.

And through all these
journeys of time,
I felt like I never walked alone
and still, I felt heavy.

1971

Voices of Whales

Islands of the world
from this open sea.
Will you speak of things
that are within me?
Listen very carefully
for their cry.

1971

Embrace of Nations

How glorious is a man's destiny
when he leaves behind
the arrows of time.
And he boldly pushes forward
through the uncertain future.

A man's destiny is glorious
because his moral error
does not doom him.
And then he survives all of his mistakes
to finally reach to this internal truth
to find that he can only draw from that.
And this is a broad enough of a ship
that draws all nations in.

We reflect in this borrowed time
so we can see the light of
one star,
one moon,
one Earth.
We can determine the extent of the ocean
because we behold one of its waves.
Deep in a soul we hide.

No Date

The Moment of Time

We live in this moral shell,
but in former existences
where each free thought
represents a home
away from home.

And this profound peace that lies
within the fullness of compassion
makes us feel like we have walked
this way before
among these beautiful trees
and along the shore
where beauty and truth
carries me into the
spangling summer sky
in a moment in time.

No Date

Will You Dance with Me?

The beginning of the wonderment of errrr
is the time when souls can begin anew.
Therefore comes the incident of terror
that I discovered while I was loving you.
With the interior forlorn
to know that I always would remember.
Turning my mind into a blue haze
that covered far too many of our days.

As I relent my inner purge
that only your smile can release.
Whatever I do from now on,
this moment will live in me forever,
burning into my brain each sunrise
because without you I am nothing.
Or so I thought.

No Date

Uncertainty I

Uncertain stride breaks.
Forever cast into echoes.
Take a moment
in a tiny blossom
if we are conscious.
Perhaps a tiny stone
in our path.
We will discover
God within.

1997

Transcending Thought

Walking between worlds
like a TV screen.
Travelling from one passage
Into the mysterious works
of our minds.
The web of transformation.
So many and yet one self.

Sharing thoughts
in some invisible mind
is taking us in circles.
The tranquil force
comforting in silence.
A gentle mist like sweet smoke,
dialing from the memory forgotten.
Breaking the silence
chambered inside flesh.

No Date

Vermont

Vermont with its transparent beauty
is the progression of chords
creating a unity of love.

All selves are woven
into the same fabric of life.
The eternal stranger.

The oak trees
experiencing immortality
bursting forth a cloud of
greenish-yellow buds.

A flowing river that begins
inside our awareness.
Expanding to create
all things and events.

I swallow its beauty,
I feel full.

2004

A Blanket of Desire

Brain cell confusion,
mind disillusion.

And the night passed
and you can see it move
into the blue blackness.

A canvas stood by the window.
It brought strange dreams
and thoughts in a mental storm.
And by the sea,
a young boy was kneeling.
His hair was made of stone,
curled by the sea salt.
And through this narrow window,
I saw a storm.
She came with a fury.

His whole life passed.
As I stood spell-bound,
he says: "There will be no storm
that matters" while he was
holding a brush on his hands.

But he's mixing the colors
in the dull of light.
It softened to burnished silver
that was reflecting the wild sea.

No Date

The Mask of Devotion

Concealing the hidden desires,
masking defensive forces,
characters in theatres
and balls in a midnight masquerade,
leading, misleading.
It's a sentiment of expression,
emotion creeping
to land a hand of devotion.

Darwin's theory of the past
is an identity of no man's mask.
Is it a fire of pain
or is it the fire of delight
taking us by the hand.

No Date

Universe in me,
Universe in You

A stranger to myself,
I got to hold on,
I got to hold on.
Stranger as strange,
silent as the breath.
Words are not always necessary
in the silence.
Winds will grow
and in the arms I will go.
Into my world I will flow
and from within my world
I experience your transcendence.

April 24, 2006

Basic energy of life

Manifesting as molecules,
super strings vibrating
at different speeds

The variations in these vibrations
produce variations in a physical matter
that makes up all things in the Universe.

December 12, 2006

Immortal

Quantum mechanics observe
that all possibilities exist.
Everything is observed
and affected by the observer.

December 25, 2006

Gypsy

Others do not paint my world.
I paint the corridors of my time.
I follow no dictators
of any belief systems.
Nor do I accept any of these.
Nor do I embrace the teaching
of any other person
for there I seek only my truth.

December 26, 2006

Work

This long journey
and in the company of a few.
My mind erupts re-awakening
of a life of fresh.

My bones and muscles
are tired of the trains, car, work.
Between pleasure and pain,
reason or hope,
All of the earthy joys,
they take shape of an illusion.

Eternal beloved.
Change is the unchangeable truth
as all things grow and fade.

No Date

Attitude

When I turn myself to you,
you assumed an air of understanding
and analyzed in terms of your
theories and ideas.
I would not say that you were objective.
In fact, quite the contrary.
Then you only see me
in your understanding

To know yourself
is to know another.
To know the other
is to know yourself.
Only then we stop searching.
Only then the journey begins.

December 17, 2001

Neus

Deep down,
somewhere in thought,
I bend down to give a praise
to my very being.

With a high impact,
I felt my body shaking.
I was extended somewhere
in between thought and time
Or is it time and space?
Nothing seem to matter
except the flight.

No Date

The Language of Music

The artist
lost
in passion.

Spirit flows
leaving body.
Mind somewhere
between concept,
a word.

Underneath the
ocean we swim.
Hunters gather
to a found
civilization.

We must
breathe,
exhale
pollution.

A giant past,
a gigantic future.

No Date

Red Hair Ghost

A chill made my bones shiver,
starring with empty sorrow,
frozen in time.
Silence,
the marble countenance of an angel
Locked in space.
A sculpture,
as light begins to fade into an October moon.

She disappears
like flowing wind
leaving a mark in stone.

Was she an angel?
Was she Eva?
Was she a ghost?
Was she me?

You send breath into spirit.
I have taken you by hand.
Lie still,
don't be afraid,
nor walk the shadowy depths.

Were the Earth to forsake you,
I shall remember you.

No Date

Nature Spirit

In bewildered streams,
lost in a musical note.

A lion stood bowing
in front of an angel.

In some corner of the world
lovers were caught.

Some mystical illusion
perhaps in some
train station's poster
hung beyond empty walls,
empty windows,
a desk in the corner,
head bowed thinking,
subdivided triangles,
a giant step confronting man.

The four corners leap
in different directions,
night and day stood still.
While the birds flew north,
the eagle flew south.

They all gathered in prayer,
young and old,
a red, white and blue ribbon,
a child playing with a kite.

Hunger,
voices known,
the blessed fish,
the promise.

Hands,
God throws down the rain
for hope.

No Date

Untitled

The serpent curled itself
up into the fresh blossoms
of Eva's breasts.

Night fell,
the moon conceived
the birth of language.

She awoke
and the sun blinded her eyes.
She looked down
and the serpent's poison
was the blood she smelled.
She rooted down
into the ground for comfort
and there she brought forth
the breath of life.

No Date

O Sun

She gently descends
from the river.
Watch as the mist
moves through her hair.
A translucent candle.

Burning in the open air
she whispers the words
and lifts invisible hands
as his garment falls
through a blazing light.

Fiercely exquisite eyes
penetrate to the center
of an open circle of flesh.
Sadness is a fire
in the clear eyes of a child.

Rippling through memories,
running toward light,
she raised his arm
with a keen sensation
frightening time
beyond the vast, empty space.

No Date

Royalty

Bodies of flesh,
government of kingdoms,
books that bound
rounding their backs
to completeness.

Retrieving one's self
into revelation
or apocalypse.
A parish festival,
a waking moment.
Wondrous manifestation
as tears rained from their eyes,
repenting the roar of lightening.

Peeking through the open window,
my dreamy body carried me
at the edge of the open door
and the sweet smell gently touched my face.

No Date

Uncertainty II

We strive to grasp
negative misunderstandings
that rest upon diversity,
between ego and illusion.

Emptiness escapes through
the walls that man built.
Monuments of logic,
enchanted gardens
carved in jewels
that hides behind a smoky cloud.

Hour passes,
parades run through,
but inner light is frightened.

No Date

Time Lapse

To pierce the mind arriving
at the internal journeys
of mind...that hurts us all.

Illusions to be discovered
that were hidden in the pendulum clock.
Tones to be awakened
that were hidden in the magical circle.
These frighten me and I despair
of imagination's power.

We are complete, but forgotten.

No Date

The Beholder's Eye

Did we see creation?
Female trees lose
their wings
through the lower sky.

The sleeping town,
souls perfumed
in blue rose.

Down the magical bottom
where fish swim,
the waters gently flow,
tiny rocks make
the way on hillsides.

The predators prey
in binocular eyes
while we cover the
flesh with
an apron of
life.

No Date

Blue Brain

The neural energy's
super human phantom
of life and death inspires us to master
the possibilities of science,
perfecting the world into revolutionary momentum.

Are we hiding in this darkness?
Are we shooting for the light -
that lays in eons of wounded souls?

Imagine us with heighten intelligence-
wrapped in the blue.
Will we fit in our world view?
Is this the journey of our souls?
Perhaps this is sealed in spirit gene
in some distant future.

Predisposed pleasure lays in the brain.
We are disciple of ship technologies,
discovering another jewel or a mandala.
The human evolution-

the archetypes of enlightened minds,
venturing into unknown.
Is it the mind or is it the thinker?

I love the empty space so I can play with perception.

Let us freely roam into this void.

We can color our blue brain in profound wisdom,
drunk with emotion.

No Date

ABOUT THE AUTHOR

Sosé Gjelaj was born in Montenegro. She relocated to the United States with her family in 1969 and has lived in America since then. Sosé is an author, a philanthropist, a published poet and a pronoun artist who had spent a lifetime studying Eastern and Western philosophy. She has academic background in Arts and is the owner of "Sosé Art Gallery" located in Bennington, VT. Sosé is the founder the "Source of Visibility," a not-for-profit humanitarian and environmental organization.

OTHER BOOKS BY THE AUTHOR

NOUN=VERB by Sosé Gjelaj and Elitsa Teneva

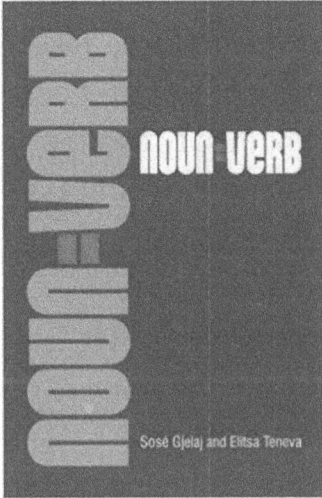

Based on over 250 research articles, Noun=Verb explores the fundamental reasons for the staggering rates of psychological disorders, violence, incarceration, failure to graduate, unemployment, suicide and exploitation among humanity. Findings demonstrate that maladjustment and trauma are not accidental. Rather, such events are deliberately orchestrated by various governmental sectors (i.e. educational system; public and mental health; judicial system) relying on an array of harmful methods (i.e. fear appeals; punishment). The goal is the acquisition of absolute corporate profit at the expense of life. Solving the injustice would require awareness and the courage to cultivate and implement a value system founded on spirituality (i.e., focus on creativity; love; autonomy; reaching one's maximum potential; positive emotions) and not on self-serving corporate interest.

SOVEREIGN TERRA by Sosé Gjelaj and Elitsa Teneva

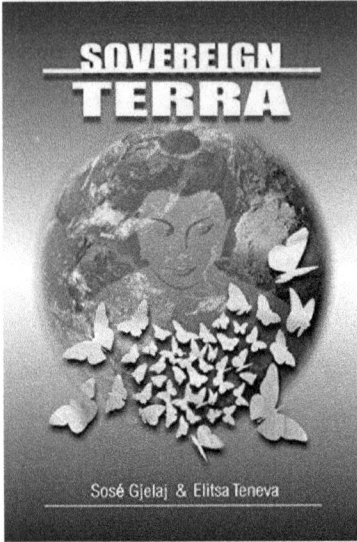

Based on a theory devised by Sosé Gjelaj and with the support of 445 peer-reviewed scientific articles, "Sovereign Terra" takes a revolutionary perspective on the state of humanity and the environment and the root cause of human disease and environmental degradation. Human and environmental deterioration are the product of a secretive agenda designed by governmental and industrial enterprises to acquire absolute profit and power at the expense of human life and environmental wellness. While humanity is deceived to believe that all care is taken by key officials to ameliorate the ever-accelerating human and environmental destruction, in truth, all planning and action is undertaken to destruct the human race and Earth. Humanity and Earth are on the verge of grand-scale collapse whether manifested through environmental disaster, human disease outbreaks or the combination of both.

We can no longer depend on those we elect to save us and our environment if we are to thrive and ensure that future generations breathe fresh air, drink clean water and consume food free of chemicals. We must act now and take full responsibility for ourselves and our planetary home. The longer we delay the implementation of restorative interventions, the more severely we will experience the devastating consequences of escalating deterioration. The first step to healing ourselves and Earth is awareness, the grand awakening to the truth. "Sovereign Terra" opens the eyes to the visibly invisible so we can, individually and collectively, consciously take action, save ourselves and Earth.

SYNCHRONIZATION OF DIMENSIONS by Sosé Gjelaj and Elitsa Teneva

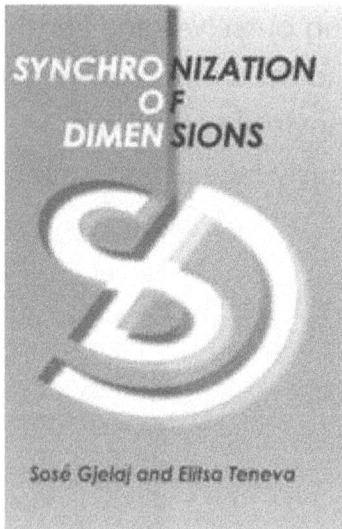

Synchronization of Dimensions takes us on a journey of the deepest questions and answers facing mankind today. Topics such as human and universally created laws, sexual energy and the difference between darkness and light are a few of the topics explored. Delving into the magic of wisdom, the reader is left with a clear understanding of his origins, spiritual makeup and genetic future.

www.ingramcontent.com/pod-product-compliance
Lightning Source LLC
Chambersburg PA
CBHW070906100426
42737CB00047B/2883

* 9 7 8 0 9 9 8 1 0 1 7 1 2 *